OLIVER CROMWELL

The Man Who Refused to be King

Written by Jonathan Bloch
In collaboration with Mathieu Beaud
Translated by Rebecca Neal

History 50MINUTES.com

OLIVER CROMWELL

KEY INFORMATION

- **Born:** 25 April 1599 in Huntingdon.
- **Died:** 3 September 1658 in London.
- **Role:** English general and Member of Parliament; Lord Protector of the Commonwealth of England, Scotland and Ireland from 1653 to his death.
- **Main achievement:** the establishment of a military junta whose conquests laid the foundation for the British Empire.

INTRODUCTION

Oliver Cromwell is undoubtedly one of the most enigmatic figures in English history. Sometimes hated, sometimes admired by different generations of historians and constantly reinvented depending on the requirements of a given context, Cromwell is a very ambiguous character. It is particularly difficult to separate the bloodthirsty tyrant from the hero who preceded him.

An austere puritan with iron discipline, Cromwell emerged from the ranks of the revolutionary army and managed to rise to the highest levels of power thanks to his unrivalled political pragmatism. He was a skilled communicator who attributed each of his military victories, no matter how small, to God, and claimed that he had been divinely chosen. Both a mystical figure and a Machiavellian genius, in 1653 Cromwell became the absolute sovereign of the British

Isles. In spite of the power he held, he refused the English crown when it was offered to him in 1657.

His political outlook was defined by fanatical idealism, which was nonetheless tempered in practice by a high degree of prudence. Although he presented himself as the champion of Protestantism and hoped to correct the population's morals and create a federation of all the Protestant nations, he managed to conclude diplomatic agreements with the Catholic powers (France and Spain).

Opinions about this complex and inexhaustible figure are likely to remain divided for many years to come.

BIOGRAPHY

Portrait of Oliver Cromwell.

BETWEEN FORTUNE AND MISFORTUNE

Cromwell was born in Huntingdon, England on 25 April 1599. Although he was a member of the gentry, he inherited next to nothing of his family's extensive wealth, which had been largely squandered by one of his grandfathers.

THE GENTRY

In England, there was a difference between noblemen, gentlemen and the middle classes. Until the 15th century, the class of gentlemen did not really exist, as these gradually appeared following the social rise of several middle-class families, who were anxious to buy their place in the nobility and attribute to themselves an illustrious, and sometimes fictitious, family tree. As such, the gentry was the order of the gentlemen, meaning nobles whose main activity was not war, but enrichment based on the ownership of land, acquired through purchase, marriage or any other arrangement. In France, this mixing between the nobility and the middle classes remained impossible during the ancien régime (1515-1789), as nobles were strictly forbidden from taking part in any commercial, industrial or entrepreneurial activity.

Forced to abandon his studies at Cambridge to take care of his mother and his seven unmarried sisters, Cromwell returned to his native region, where he married Elizabeth Bourchier (1598-1665), the daughter of a London merchant, with whom he had nine children.

During the 1620s, he fell ill and suffered from a major bout of depression. He came out of this more puritanical than ever, convinced that he was accompanied by God throughout every stage of his life, in both his misfortunes and his triumphs.

After falling into poverty, Cromwell sold almost all his property in 1631 and resolved to work on the land himself as a farmer. Five years later, he inherited a substantial amount of property from an uncle in Ely, where he moved. Now free from want and with the benefit of a large family network, he was elected to the Short Parliament in 1640, then to the Long Parliament, which was convened a few months later.

Did you know?

On 13 April 1640, Charles I (King of England, Scotland and Ireland, 1600-1649) convened the Parliament in order to raise funds. As it rejected his requests, it was dissolved less than a month later. It would later be known as the Short Parliament, in contrast to the Long Parliament, which was convened later that year and sat for two decades.

LORD PROTECTOR OF THE COMMONWEALTH

In 1640, when Cromwell was already 41 years old, there was nothing to suggest that he was destined to become ruler.

This began to change in 1641, when war broke out between Parliament and the King. That year, Cromwell distinguished himself in the ranks of the Parliamentarian army through his rigid discipline. As leader of a cavalry troop, he imposed draconian rules on his men, inspired by his puritan ethics: swearing and gambling were strictly forbidden, and the men only received recognition for their personal merits, regardless of their religious affinities.

Faced with opponents who were less organised and strict than him, Cromwell won a string of victories. He attributed them all to God, of whom he said he was merely an instrument. He was soon promoted to the rank of Lieutenant-General. More convinced than ever of the rightness of his cause, he dreamt of an England with a reformed government and way of life. Strictness and austerity were the watchwords of the programme he wanted to put forward to turn the English into the people of God.

In 1646, once Parliament had defeated Charles I, Cromwell briefly abandoned his function as a military officer to devote his full attention to the debates of the Long Parliament, which was at that time shaken by major disagreements.

He nonetheless rejoined the cavalry when Charles I managed to escape. The King immediately mobilised a new army against Parliament, but failed in this last attempt. He was imprisoned again, before being sentenced to death and executed in 1649.

Well-liked by the gentry, of which he was a member, and respected by the army, which he had led to victory on

numerous occasions, Cromwell now appeared to be the na-
tural leader of England. Between 1649 and 1651, he brutally
subdued rebellions within the British Isles, and in 1653 he
was named Lord Protector by the Long Parliament. After
becoming the unchallenged ruler of Great Britain, Cromwell
refused the crown which was offered to him in 1657 and
remained in power until his death in 1658.

He was buried in Westminster Abbey with all the honours
due to a legitimate monarch. However, as soon as the
Stuart dynasty returned to the throne in 1660, Cromwell's
body was disinterred, hanged, and beheaded, and his head
was placed on a spike above Westminster Hall for decades,
before becoming a curiosity for a wealthy collector.

Cromwell's execution.

CONTEXT

THE KING AND THE PARLIAMENT

By the start of the 17th century, the institutions of the Kingdom of England were already solid.

The king was at the highest level of the executive, judicial and legislative powers. Nonetheless, because of the Magna Carta signed in 1215 and several centuries of tradition, the king had to ask for the approval of Parliament when taking certain decisions. In particular, he could not levy additional taxes, even during times of war, without the prior mutual agreement of the House of Lords and the House of Commons.

THE MAGNA CARTA

In 1215, King John Lackland (1167-1216) granted his subjects a series of fundamental freedoms, which were all enshrined in the Magna Carta: the right to property, the right to free movement, the right to impartial justice, the right to refuse the excessive levying of taxes, etc. The role of the English Parliament, which was established in around 1300, then involved ensuring that these legal provisions were respected. However, the institution was not yet a permanent assembly, as is the case today, but an extraordinary assembly, convened and dissolved on the initiative of the king alone.

The Tudor dynasty (1485-1603), which ruled England before the Stuart dynasty (1603-1714), saw to it that Parliament was never summoned. Henry VIII (1491-1547) and Elizabeth I (1533-1603) managed to find ingenious tricks to avoid levying taxes to support their military undertakings. Henry VIII, who converted his country to Protestantism by declaring himself the sole head of the Church of England (1535), swelled his treasury by stripping the regular clergy of their possessions. Elizabeth I, a sworn enemy of King Philip II of Spain (1527-1598), encouraged state-sponsored piracy and protected corsairs who were tasked with attacking Spanish commercial lines by pillaging their galleons, which were transporting valuable commodities from the New World, in particular gold, sugar, tobacco and spices.

James I (1566-1625), who succeeded Elizabeth I, nonetheless endeavoured to re-establish friendly relations between Spain and England. To do this, he renounced state-sponsored piracy and the profits it brought. While the income of the royal estate allowed him to preserve his government and its institutions, he nonetheless had to rely on additional taxes and, therefore, on the support of Parliament for any costly undertakings. His son, Charles I, had to do the same. However, this situation was in conflict with the ambition of the Stuarts, who wanted to establish themselves as an absolutist dynasty by divine right.

TWO DIFFERENT PARLIAMENTARY SYSTEMS

The English Parliament and the French *parlements* of the ancien régime were two entirely different kinds of institution. Whereas the English Parliament is a representative assembly of the British people, the French *parlements* under the ancien régime were courts of sovereign justice, where justice was dispensed on behalf of the king. However, there was a representative assembly comparable to the British Parliament in ancien régime France: the Estates-General.

While the British Parliament was – and still is – divided into two houses (the House of Lords, historically for the nobility, and the House of Commons, historically for the common people), the Estates-General in France had only one chamber, where the representatives were divided into three orders (nobility, clergy and the Third Estate).

In the Estates-General, there were equal numbers of representatives for the nobility, clergy and Third Estate, without any proportional relationship to the composition of the French population. The representation of the people was therefore very unequal and favourable to the elites. Conversely, in the Parliament in England, the House of Commons progressively acquired more rights, until it made the House of Lords almost obsolete. However, the House of Lords did not disappear, and even until 2009 was the highest court of justice in England.

ANGLICANISM: AN ORIGINAL SYNTHESIS OF CATHOLICISM AND CALVINISM

Protestantism, as it was practiced in England at the start of the 17th century, was unique. The king had been the sole head of the Church since the Act of Supremacy passed by Henry VIII in 1534. This Anglican Church, which had no monasteries or convents, divided the country into dioceses placed under the authority of bishops.

However, following the Thirty-Nine Articles of Religion put forward under the reign of Elizabeth I in 1563, the Church of England was heavily influenced by the doctrine of John Calvin (French Protestant pastor and founder of Calvinism, 1509-1564). Calvin thought that each believer was a priest due to the doctrine of universal priesthood. As such, the subordination of the faithful to parish priests and the subordination of parish priests to bishops was an aberration according to Calvinist thought. Nonetheless, this hierarchy still existed within the Church of England.

Anglicanism therefore borrowed some elements from Calvinism, such as the complete lack of ornamentation in places of worship and religious services in the vernacular language (as Catholic Mass was delivered in Latin). In addition, both branches recognised the principle of predestination. According to this postulate, God had decided from Creation to save only a few chosen people. Consequently, man no longer had to live in fear of being saved or punished, as his fate had been decided before he was born. It was nonetheless supposed that the chosen ones would recognise themselves in the joy they felt in working. This, together with the fact that Calvinist doctrine allowed loans with interest, meant that Calvinism and Anglicanism naturally favoured bourgeois industrial capitalism.

THE GRADUAL COLLAPSE OF ANGLICANISM

Over time, Anglicanism was influenced by different religious ideologies, which fractured its fragile unity. As such, different groups, which could even be described as sects, emerged, and were preoccupied as much with questions of faith as with politics. During the first half of the 17th century, Arminians and Puritans clashed on the chessboard of power.

English Arminianism differed from the movement as it appeared in the Netherlands at the beginning of the 17th century. Jakob Hermanszoon, called Jacobus Arminius (1560-1609), a Dutch theologian and minister in the Protestant Church, had in his time questioned the principle of predetermination and, like his compatriot Erasmus (Dutch humanist, 1469-1536) before him, believed that man was free to accept or reject the grace of God, which is offered to all rather than to a handful of chosen ones. In England, the Arminians, who were only a small minority of clerics, wanted, beyond the theological debate, the restoration of embellished and regulated religious practices. This outraged the Puritans. As the Puritans preached obedience to the king, they received the support of Charles I. Disagreements between the two groups were exacerbated in 1633, when the Archbishop of Canterbury William Laud (1573-1645), who had been won over by Arminianism, organised a series of reforms that opponents saw as a Catholic threat.

While the Arminians tended to strengthen the Catholic aspect of Anglicanism, the Puritans were fervent defenders of its Calvinist side. For Puritans, adoration of God should be felt at every moment in life, not just at certain times. In addition, they followed a very strict lifestyle and their churches were devoid of any ornamentation. At the start of the 17th century, the movement in England split into Presbyterians and independents. The former, who were often wealthy landowners, recommended a unified and standardised national Church, whereas the latter, who were fewer in number but no less influential, believed that the worship of God should be independent of any state supervision.

THE UNSUCCESSFUL REIGN OF CHARLES I

Charles I, King of Britain from 1625 onwards, did not manage to unite the different factions that were fighting for political and religious power, or to overcome their disagreements. Conversely, his policy of favouritism intensified the frustrations of the parties, whose feeling that they had been wronged led them to form an opposition and seek immediate confrontation.

Attracted by the principle of absolute monarchy as practiced in the Catholic countries of France and Spain, Charles I promoted reforms that brought Anglicanism closer to Roman Catholicism, despite the vocal alarm of his Puritan subjects. When Archbishop Laud undertook his Arminian reforms from 1633, people made their concerns heard in Scotland. The Scots, most of whom were Presbyterian, saw any formalisation of the ecclesiastical hierarchy as contrary to their values, according to the principle of universal priesthood. In 1639, they rebelled against ecclesiastical and royal authority with the aim of establishing a national Presbyterian Church.

HIGHLIGHTS

THE CIVIL WAR

Adding fuel to the fire (1640-1641)

The Scottish insurrection in favour of Presbyterianism and the abolition of any ecclesiastical hierarchy in 1639 forced Charles I to raise an army that he did not have the funds for. Consequently, he convened Parliament in April 1640. However, he was unable to get along with it and dissolved it, and reached an agreement with the rebels. His prestige was tarnished as a result, and he still did not have the funds he needed. On 3 November 1640, he convened Parliament again. Cromwell attended both sessions.

While a political power struggle pitted the King against his Parliament, in particular on the subject of the nomination of his ministers and the management of his institutions, a new revolt broke out in October 1641, this time in Ireland. Since the rise to power of the Tudor dynasty, the Irish had seen their land confiscated and redistributed for the benefit of British magnates. The religious differences between this Catholic country and Protestant England did nothing to improve the situation.

Charles I therefore sent an army to deal with the problem. Parliament immediately demanded control of this army and, after this demand was rejected, decided to raise its own troops. The King was then forced to abandon the war in Ireland to do battle against the representative assembly.

The Ironsides (1641-1644)

Cromwell decided to enter the ranks of the Parliamentarian army at his own expense. He gathered Puritan volunteers who were just as pious as him and provided them with horses, war material and crossbows, and subjected them to very harsh discipline. By favouring hand-to-hand combat and carrying out an increasing number of compact and large-scale charges, they broke through the enemy ranks, which splintered apart.

After joining the Eastern Association under the command of Edward Montagu, 2nd Earl of Manchester (1602-1671) in 1643, Cromwell and his men distinguished themselves at the Battle of Marston Moor (2 July 1644). During this battle, Prince Rupert of the Rhine (1619-1682), the commander of Charles I's troops, gave them the impressive nickname of 'Ironsides'. Although Cromwell had no military experience, he was now a rising star among the officers of the Parliamentarian army. Frustrated by the lack of zeal of the Earl of Manchester, whom he suspected of having Royalist sympathies, he advocated stripping him of his post in the strongest possible terms before Parliament in November 1644.

Cromwell at the Battle of Marston Moor, c. 1877.

From the New Model Army to the Rump Parliament (1645-1649)

In 1645, in order to force the Earl of Manchester out of the army, Cromwell proposed a law which would forbid

Members of Parliament from taking part in military activities. The law was passed and all officers from the House of Lords were removed from their posts, including Cromwell himself. However, his friend Thomas Fairfax (English general, 1612-1671) immediately applied for a special exemption for the Puritan gentleman, whose skills as a cavalry leader were deemed indispensable. Parliament granted the exception, putting Cromwell in a unique and highly advantageous situation, as he was now the only person taking part in both the political debates and the military decision-making.

That same year, Cromwell and Fairfax set up the New Model Army. Thanks to this new army, Cromwell won a number of victories, some of which proved decisive and ensured the military triumph of the Long Parliament over the English monarchy.

Unlike in the past, the soldiers in the New Model Army were recruited on a national rather than a regional basis. They therefore came from all over England, and their mission was no longer to only defend their own region, but to take part in campaigns across the whole country. They were subjected to the same puritanical discipline as the Ironsides and had the best information network of the time. United by a republican ideal, they favoured an economic model involving the sharing of resources. The most radical among them proposed not only the abolition of the monarchy, but the destruction of any form of aristocracy. These men were known as Levellers, and the most extreme of them were known as Diggers.

The Levellers believed that the power of the aristo-cratic elites was a tyrannical usurpation whose origins could be traced back to the submission of England by William the Conqueror (Duke of Normandy and King of England, 1028-1087) in 1066. This idea would persist among radical political groups until the 18th century. This is why the Levellers thought that the country's resources should be fairly distributed among all its inhabitants, in order to restore a lost golden age. However, their organisation remained very unstable and their connections in civil society and the army were so cowardly that they gave way to the slightest form of repression.

The Levellers also counted among their ranks some fanatics with whom they categorically refused to be associated: the Diggers. The Diggers, who formed a kind of sect, thought that a violent revolution was the only way to achieve their ends. Some even tried to assassinate Cromwell after he had become Lord Protector, as they saw him as a traitor to the ideals that had justified a civil war against the King. According to their logic, once Cromwell became sovereign he was no better than the monarch he had replaced. The Diggers established themselves in small, independent agricul-tural communities scattered across England. These communities were harshly repressed, until they were completely eradicated in 1650.

In the short-to-medium-term, Cromwell's law and the creation of the New Model Army caused Parliament and the army to split into two rival political bodies. The ideology of the assembly, where the majority were Presbyterian, was completely different to that shared by the republican soldiers. The Presbyterians, who were mainly members of the gentry, were staunchly opposed to the abolition of the right to property. In addition, after Charles I was captured after the Battle of Naseby (14 June 1645), they proposed de-mobilising the army without paying the soldiers the wages they were owed. Cromwell was now forced to manage a conflict between factions which threatened the unity of the revolutionary movement.

He therefore decided to persecute the Diggers and repress the Levellers, thus purging his army of its most dangerous elements. At the same time, he organised a major reorga-nisation of Parliament in December 1648 to make it more sympathetic, and even more submissive, to the demands of the army. This elimination was carried out at the request of the army, and had no legal basis.

The end of the Second Civil War (1649)

In 1645, Charles I was captured after his defeat at the Battle of Naseby by the New Model Army. However, in 1647 he escaped and took refuge on the Isle of Wight, from where he managed to mobilise a Scottish army. This army was crushed by Cromwell at the Battle of Preston in 1648. Charles I was brought back to London by force and, as his escape was considered to be treason towards the British people, he was sentenced to death by Parliament. Although

Cromwell had for a long time thought that the power of the monarchy was indispensable in England, Charles I's escape altered his opinion. He therefore also called for the death penalty, and Charles I was beheaded in front of the Palace of Whitehall on 27 January 1649. The Stuart dynasty was thus removed from the throne, and the monarchy was abolished. Cromwell became the most important man in England, and soon he would be the unchallenged ruler.

THE COMMONWEALTH AND THE PROTECTORATE

Toward the legitimisation of power (1649-1659)

During the Commonwealth (1649-1653) and the Protectorate (1653-1659), Cromwell tried in vain to legitimise his power through legal means. However, Britain remained a military junta with a formidable administration, held together by an inflexible Puritanism. Parliament underwent a number of difficult changes and struggled to establish itself as a real political force. It was chained down, subjected to a series of purges and perfectly controlled by Cromwell, who removed all his opponents from it. He drew his power from his military and religious charisma, and from the mythical aura surrounding his person.

From 1650 to 1658, England was essentially a well-disguised dictatorship. Power was mainly exercised by the Council of State, which comprised 41 incorruptible men. They all supported Cromwell's dictatorship, and proved so effective that Parliament was powerless in the management of government affairs.

The military also occupied a powerful position in this English state that was constantly at war with its neighbours. As the political structures of the Commonwealth were now obsolete, in 1653 Cromwell's generals drew up the Instrument of Government. This, the first constitutional text in the history of the Western world, gave Cromwell the title of Lord Protector, thus raising him to the status of sovereign of England.

With the establishment of the Protectorate, a new Parliament was convened. It tried to revise the different clauses of the Instrument of Government, to the great displeasure of Cromwell, who dissolved it. When it was convened for the second time in 1657, Parliament once again revised the constitutional text, but this time tried to pander to the Lord Protector. The Humble Petition and Advice even offered him the crown, which he prudently rejected. However, he accepted other points, in particular the restoration of a bicameral parliament, as the House of Lords had effectively been abolished since the establishment of the Commonwealth. This was now replaced by another chamber known as the Other House.

Cromwell dissolves Parliament.

The brutal subjection of Ireland and Scotland (1649-1652)

Shortly after the establishment of the Commonwealth and the abolition of the monarchy, Cromwell was sent to Ireland by Parliament in order to resolve the situation of anarchy that had prevailed there since the insurrection of 1641. On 11 September 1649, he conquered Drogheda, the headquarters of the resistance. When the garrison of the town refused to surrender even though it did not have the means to win, Cromwell ordered that the entire population be put to the sword, claiming that this was God's will.

After Ireland had been brutally repressed, Cromwell

embarked on the conquest of Scotland, which had chosen to recognise Charles II (1630-1685) rather than side with the revolutionaries of the Commonwealth. Cromwell triumphed in rapid succession over the Scottish armies at the Battle of Dunbar on 3 September 1650, and then a year later at the Battle of Worcester. Ireland and Scotland were definitively integrated into the new regime and peace was guaranteed until the death of the Lord Protector. By now, no faction dared take up arms, as the New Model Army and the Ironsides had provided conclusive proof of their strength.

Cromwell at Dunbar, painting by Andrew Carrick Gow, 1886.

The triumph of the British Empire (1652-1657)

Once the British Isles were unified under Cromwell's leadership, the country could finally turn its attention to the international scene and oversee its interests there. Cromwell, who dreamed of a great union of the Protestant nations, nonetheless proved unable to bring this project to fruition.

Perhaps idealistic, but above all pragmatic, he took Britain to war against the United Provinces (the modern-day Netherlands) for imperialistic and economic reasons. He was also suspicious of Sweden, which remained the traditional leader of the Protestant nations in Europe. Eventually, it was with the Catholic powers that Cromwell actually managed to conclude diplomatic agreements. After trying to establish good relations with Spain, he entered into a military alliance with France to the detriment of Spain and ensured the conquest of Dunkirk.

The First Anglo-Dutch War (1652-1654)

While England was embroiled in internal conflicts, the United Provinces took advantage of this to boost their maritime trade. This small Calvinist nation, which had only just freed itself from Spanish domination, was now a world leader in overseas trade. The Dutch navy sailed across the entire world, and the Dutch East India Company reaped enormous profits.

However, Cromwell was not happy that his neighbours across the Channel were trading freely with the British colonies in America, because that interfered with his imperialist ambitions. A violent conflict at sea ensured, which the British won in 1654. From that point on, England's trading monopoly over its North American colonies was ensured. However, the market of the Spanish colonies in South America remained closed.

The conquests of Jamaica (1654) and Dunkirk (1657)

To ensure total hegemony, Britain needed to measure up to France and Spain, its two rivals who were themselves at war with one another. Since France refused to recognise the legitimacy of the Commonwealth, Cromwell would have preferred to secure an alliance with Spain. He therefore went against the nation of the young Louis XIV (1638-1715), whose government was led by Cardinal Mazarin (1602-1661), who was continuing the political work of Cardinal Richelieu (1585-1642). However, during negotiations, Spain categorically refused to allow England to trade with its South American colonies. On the back of his victory over the United Provinces, Cromwell proceeded to invade Hispaniola (an island in the Caribbean; present-day Haiti and Dominican Republic). This incursion failed, but in 1654 the English managed to take over Jamaica and establish a solid outpost in the Caribbean.

Mazarin was impressed by Cromwell's aggressive policy and decided to form a military alliance with him against Spain. Furthermore, both countries agreed to refrain from providing aid to their respective rebels. Consequently, Charles II was driven out of France, where he had taken refuge.

England and France raised a coalition army to attack the Spanish Netherlands and laid siege to Dunkirk. This port city on the Channel was taken on 25 June 1568 and given to the English. This was Cromwell's last triumph, and he died a few months later, in September.

IMPACT

THE CONSOLIDATION OF THE FOUNDATIONS OF THE BRITISH COLONIAL EMPIRE

During the reigns of James I and Charles I, England had experienced something of a recession as a colonial empire. The desire of the first Stuarts to avoid any excessively costly conflict with Spain, as well as their lack of competitiveness with regard to the United Provinces, had severely reduced the kingdom's naval potential which had been raised by Elizabeth I.

Cromwell fully restored England's naval prestige, to the point that it became the leading maritime power in the West. Despite the exploits of the New Model Army on land, it was through its fleet that Britain made its mark on the international scene. Although it did not yet have a foothold in India, it nonetheless consolidated its position in the Atlantic by conquering Jamaica and by ensuring its economic monopoly over its American colonies. In doing so, it strengthened the foundations of its vast future colonial empire. England thus became a fully-fledged maritime nation, and the momentum created by Cromwell's government would not be impeded when the Stuarts returned to the throne.

THE RESTORATION OF THE TRADITIONAL MONARCHY

The Protectorate did not endure for long after Cromwell's death. His son Richard (1626-1712), who succeeded him, lacked his charisma. He had no military victories to his name, and the generals were suspicious of him and, to an even greater extent, the influence of civilian officers on him. Just a few months after he came to power, he was overthrown in a coup d'état, led by his generals who went to war against each other.

Charles II, who was abroad at this stage, seized the opportunity to claim his throne. Former generals of Oliver Cromwell, who were determined to restore order and legality to England, decided to support his cause. In February 1660, they reinstated the Long Parliament as it was before Cromwell's purge. Shortly afterwards, the assembly voted for its own dissolution and called for free elections. In April, a Convention Parliament (meaning a Parliament that had not been called by a sovereign) was formed. On 8 May, the Convention Parliament recognised Charles II as the legitimate monarch of the Kingdom of Britain. The country, which was still traumatised by the painful memory of the Civil War, jubilantly welcomed the Restoration.

Most of Cromwell's legislative reforms were overturned. Furthermore, his strict policies with regard to morality and customs were discarded: all the old vices and pleasures, including theatre, gambling and prostitution, were re-established.

CROMWELL'S LEGACY

In terms of its programme, Cromwell's government was a failure. Although he aspired to a major reform of the population's way of life and wanted to make the English the people of God, Puritanism did not take root in the hearts of citizens. In the same way, in spite of the Lord Protector's dream of unifying the Protestant nations, the opposite happened. For example, Sweden, which was already the leader of the Protestant nations, stubbornly refused to base its decision-making on British policy. For their part, the United Provinces preferred to declare war on London's imperialist ambitions. This left Cromwell with no choice but to go to war with them, in spite of the holy unity he was hoping for.

Nonetheless, in terms of results, Cromwell's regime was one of the most effective in history. When England, Ireland and Scotland were entangled in endless factional struggles, he managed to restore peace, public order and unity. Of course, he used force to achieve this, but he is far from the only leader to have done so.

In doing this, the Lord Protector established an almost invincible land army and restored the prestige of the English navy through his merciless triumph over the Dutch fleet. In this way, he managed to turn the English forces outwards and ensured the conquests of Jamaica and Dunkirk. A skilled strategist and politician, he overcame the differences between France and Spain to give his country a leading role on the international stage. However, his legacy is tarnished by the fact that his government was more like a military junta than a constitutional state. For all that, he remains an incredibly interesting figure who will no doubt continue to be discussed for a long time to come.

SUMMARY

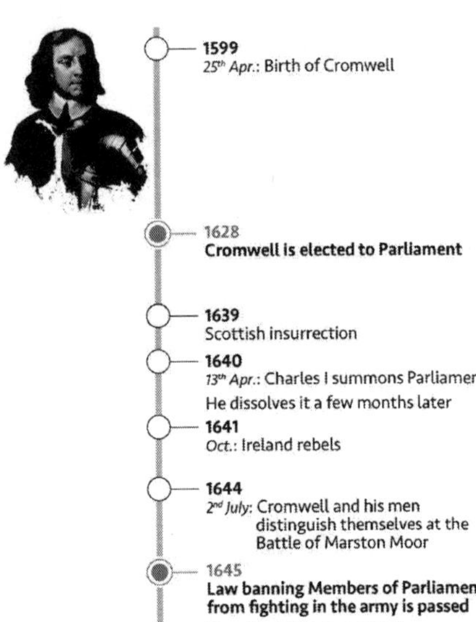

1599
25ᵗʰ Apr.: Birth of Cromwell

1628
Cromwell is elected to Parliament

1639
Scottish insurrection

1640
13ᵗʰ Apr.: Charles I summons Parliament
He dissolves it a few months later

1641
Oct.: Ireland rebels

1644
2ⁿᵈ July: Cromwell and his men
distinguish themselves at the
Battle of Marston Moor

1645
**Law banning Members of Parliament
from fighting in the army is passed**

New Model Army created

14ᵗʰ June: Charles I is captured during
the Battle of Naseby

1647
Charles I escapes

1648
Dec.: **Cromwell organises a purge of Parliament**

1649
27ᵗʰ Jan.: Execution of Charles I

Ireland is subdued

1650-1653
Commonwealth

1652
Scotland is subdued

1653
Parliament names Cromwell Lord Protector

1653-1658
Protectorate

1657
Cromwell refuses the English crown

1658
3ʳᵈ Sept.: Death of Cromwell

1660
Feb.: Long Parliament reinstated

8ᵗʰ May: Convention Parliament recognises Charles II as legitimate sovereign

- In 1640, Charles I convened Parliament in order to obtain funds to raise an army against Scotland. However, Parliament refused to grant this to him without a series of changes to the government in return. As the King found these changes unacceptable, he dealt with the Scots directly to restore order.

- As the situation was calming down in Scotland, another

insurrection took place in Ireland. Charles I was infuriated and once again summoned Parliament.

- As the King sent an army to put an end to the Irish insurrection, Parliament voted to raise its own army and refused to dissolve. This marked the beginning of the English Civil War, and Charles I was forced to leave London.
- Oliver Cromwell, a Member of Parliament, used his own money to recruit a cavalry regiment for the Parliamentarian army. He quickly established strict discipline within the ranks of his troops. Furthermore, he only distinguished his men based on their genuine merit, regardless of their faith (they were nonetheless all Protestant).
- Convinced that he was acting according to the will of God, Cromwell was unhappy at being held back by superiors who were less zealous than him, such as the 2nd Earl of Manchester. In 1644, he openly criticised the Earl before the House of Commons and had a law passed to prevent Members of Parliament from serving in the army. Although Cromwell should also have been affected by this law, he received a special dispensation.
- At the same time, he played an active part in setting up the New Model Army, which allowed the Parliamentarians to secure a first victory over the King at the Battle of Naseby in 1645.
- Parliament and the army quickly turned into two rival political bodies which disagreed as to how the revolution should be managed. Parliament proposed dissolving the New Model Army, but Cromwell could not accept this and purged the Parliament of his opponents.

- Meanwhile, Charles I escaped and raised a new army in Scotland to support his cause. However, this army was defeated by Cromwell. Captured and found guilty of treason, Charles I was executed in 1649. His heir, Charles II, was denied access to the throne, and England became a republic known as the Commonwealth in 1650. The Commonwealth was soon replaced by the Protectorate (1653), at which point Cromwell became the true ruler of the British Isles.
- Between 1649 and 1652, he used military force to subdue Ireland and Scotland.
- Once order had been restored in Britain, the country went to war against the United Provinces in order to assure its trading monopoly over its American colonies. War raged at sea between the two Protestant nations from 1652 to 1654.
- As Spain refused to grant England the right to trade with its South American colonies, Cromwell decided to invade Hispaniola. Although the island resisted the British assault, Jamaica was captured in 1654. This success improved diplomatic relations with France, which was at that time at war with Spain, and the two nations joined forces. This military alliance culminated in the conquest of Dunkirk in 1657.
- The same year, the second Parliament of the Protectorate proposed a revision of the constitutional text underpinning the regime through the Humble Petition and Advice. This offered Cromwell the crown, which he refused, although he did agree to re-establish a bicameral system in Parliament.
- Cromwell died in 1658. His son Richard succeeded him,

but was soon overthrown by his father's former officers. Some of them called Charles II back to prevent the country from falling into chaos. As soon as he acceded to the throne, Charles II abolished all the measures taken by the Lord Protector. The parliamentary monarchy was fully restored and Cromwell's name was blackened by Royalist propaganda.

We want to hear from you!
Leave a comment on your online library
and share your favourite books on social media!

FIND OUT MORE

BIBLIOGRAPHY

- Abbott, W.C. (1937-1947) *The Writings and Speeches of Oliver Cromwell*. Cambridge, Massachusetts: Harvard University Press.
- Ashley, M. (1972) *Oliver Cromwell and His World*. London: Thames & Hudson.
- BCW Project (No date) *Homepage*. [Online]. [Accessed 23 February 2017]. Available from: <http://bcw-project.org/>
- Brown, P.H. (1962) *A Short History of Scotland*. London: Oliver & Boyd.
- Cottret, B. (1992) *Cromwell*. Paris: Fayard.
- Coward, B. (1991) *Oliver Cromwell*. London: Longman.
- Davies, G. (1959) *The Oxford History of England: The Early Stuarts*, volume 9. Oxford: Clarendon Press.
- Davies, J. (1993) *A History of Wales*. London: Penguin.
- Firth, C. (1900) *Oliver Cromwell and the Rule of the Puritans*. London: G.P. Putnam's Sons.
- Firth, C. (1909) *The Last Years of the Protectorate*. London: Longman.
- Firth, C. (2005) *Cromwell's Army*. Boston, Massachusetts: Elibron Classics.
- Gardiner, S.R. (1882) *History of England from the Accession of King James I to the Outbreak of the Civil War*. London/New York: Longman-Green.
- Guy, J. and Morrill, J. (1992) *The Oxford History of Britain: The Tudors and Stuarts*, volume 3. Oxford: Oxford University Press.

- Hirst, D. (1986) *Authority and Conflict: England 1603-1658*. Cambridge, Massachusetts: Harvard University Press.
- Moody, T.W., Martin, F.X. and Byrne, F.J. (1978) *A New History of Ireland: Early Modern Ireland (1534-1691)*, volume 3. Oxford: Clarendon Press.
- Morgan, K.O. (1984) *The Oxford Illustrated History of Britain*. Oxford: Oxford University Press.
- Morrill, J. (1990) *Oliver Cromwell and the English Revolution*. New York: Longman.
- Morrill, J. (1992) *Revolution and Restoration: England in the 1650s*. London: Collins & Brown.
- Newman, P.R. (1990) *Companion to the English Civil Wars*. London: Facts on File.
- Reid, S. (2004) *Dunbar 1650: Cromwell's Most Famous Victory*. Oxford: Osprey Publishing.
- Stevenson, D. (2003) *The Scottish Revolution 1637-1644: The Triumph of the Covenanters*. Edinburgh: John Donald.
- Wheeler, J.S. (1999) *Cromwell in Ireland*. New York: St Martin's Press.
- Woolrych, A. (2000) *Commonwealth and Protectorate*. London: Phoenix Press.
- Worden, B. (1977) *The Rump Parliament*. Cambridge: Cambridge University Press.

ADDITIONAL SOURCES

- Barratt, J. (2006) *Cromwell's Wars at Sea*. Barnsley: Pen & Sword.
- Braddick, M. (2008) *God's Fury, England's Fire: A New History of the English Civil Wars*. London: Allen Lane.

- Bradstock, A. (2011) *Radical Religion in Cromwell's England*. London: I.B. Tauris.
- Davies, G. (1955) *The Restoration of Charles II, 1658-1660*. San Marino: Huntingdon Library.
- Edwards, G. (1999) *The Last Days of Charles I*. Stroud: Sutton Publishing.
- Gregg, P. (1984) *King Charles I*. Berkeley: University of California Press.
- Hoile, D. (1992) *The Levellers: Libertarian Radicalism and the English Civil War*. London: Libertarian Alliance.
- Hutton, R. (1989) *Charles II, King of England, Scotland and Ireland*. Oxford: Oxford University Press.

ICONOGRAPHIC SOURCES

- Portrait of Oliver Cromwell. Royalty-free reproduction picture.
- Cromwell's execution. Royalty-free reproduction picture.
- Cromwell at the Battle of Marston Moor, c. 1877. Royalty-free reproduction picture.
- Cromwell dissolves Parliament. Royalty-free reproduction picture.
- *Cromwell at Dunbar*, painting by Andrew Carrick Gow, 1886. Royalty-free reproduction picture.

FILMS

- Cromwell. (1970) [Film]. Ken Hughes. Dir. United Kingdom: Columbia Pictures.

LITERATURE

- Dumas, A. (2008) *Twenty Years After*. Oxford: Oxford University Press.
- Scott, W. (2015) *Woodstock*. CreateSpace Independent Publishing Platform.

COMMEMORATIVE BUILDINGS

- The Cromwell Museum, Huntingdon (United Kingdom).
- Statue of Oliver Cromwell, designed by Hamo Thornycroft, Westminster (London).

IMPROVE YOUR GENERAL KNOWLEDGE

IN A BLINK OF AN EYE !

www.50minutes.com

www.50minutes.com

Ebook EAN: 9782806290199

Paperback EAN: 9782806294234

Legal Deposit: D/2017/12603/96

Cover: © Primento

Digital conception by Primento, the digital partner of publishers.